PRAISE FOR

THE VICAR OF TENT TOWN

In *The Vicar of Tent Town*, the Rev. Shauna Hyde tells the story of her calling to what most would consider a rather unusual ministry. Newly called to a Charleston, WV United Methodist church, she is introduced by members of her own congregation to a homeless encampment, and in the course of the story she becomes its Vicar – the pastor for the homeless, even as she served a traditional congregation. In the course of this insightful book by Shauna Hyde we are drawn into her ministry, getting to know both members of her congregation who encouraged her in this ministry and who shared in it with her. We also get to know the residents of this community, discovering that there are many reasons why people end up homeless and why they stay homeless. You might be surprised at what you learn. This is not only a book that informs; it inspires one to new visions of ministry. In a time when religion is seen as irrelevant to life, Shauna Hyde offers evidence to the contrary.

Robert D. Cornwall
Pastor, Central Woodward Christian Church
(Disciples of Christ)
Troy, MI

John Wesley, the founder of Methodism believed that holiness is "perfect love of God and neighbor" and "there is no holiness that is not social holiness." Shauna Hyde is what the historians calls "one of Mr. Wesley's preachers." I believe that John Wesley is proud of the vicar of tent town.

This is a book that you will love. Shauna Hyde weaves the strands of her relationships with three remarkable men, Charlie, Robert and Noah, through the fabric of tent town.

This is really a devotional book. It will move you to prayer, and to increase your own commitment to social holiness, to perfect love of God and neighbor.

William Boyd Grove
Bishop, Retired, United Methodist Church

Rev. Shauna Hyde, also lovingly known as Rev BadAss, takes us on a journey through vignettes and scenes from her life as a pastor to ALL God's children ... young and old, gay and straight, housed and unhoused, rich and poor, hungry and well-fed. Hers is not a one-dimensional ministry, as she follows the lead of Jesus into unexpected sectors of our society. As someone who works to help the United Methodist Church become more inclusive and welcoming to the lesbian, gay, bisexual and transgender (LGBT) community, I am especially encouraged that she lovingly provokes the reader to consider their own response to the LGBT community. She tells the story of her own journey around acceptance in a way that is inviting and full of hope.

Helen Ryde
Regional Organizer - Southeastern Jurisdiction
Reconciling Ministries Network

The *Vicar of Tent Town* is eye opening and heart changing. I had the privilege to welcome the author in Charleston at the local soup kitchen where I worked. Many days we walked the blocks between our offices to discuss our concerns, pray and look for solutions for those who were experiencing homelessness, hunger, mental illness and more. Shauna quickly fell in love with the people of Charleston and now the people of Ravenswood, WV. Her stories of Noah, Robert and Charlie, befriending the residents of Tent Town, the essays and how a refrigerator is helping combat hunger will bring laughter, tears and maybe conviction that opens your eyes to see your community with new eyes – God's eyes. Every Tent Town needs a Vicar like Shauna!

Rhondell Miller
Executive Director of HOTEL INC, Bowling Green KY

For Shauna Hyde, the Christian life is not about following the rules; it is about following Jesus. In this series of poignant reflections on her efforts to do just that, *The Vicar of Tent Town* asks the tough questions about faithful living: What separates us from God and from each other? How do we find grace and love in the midst of pain, loss, and brokenness? What does redemption look like? While Hyde does not have all the answers, she can testify to the holiness of chaotic community, radical hospitality, and unexpected, life changing relationships. From a broken cigarette to an outdoor fridge, this book offers readers stirring images of what Christian ministry can and should look like.

Adam Ployd
Assistant Professor of Church History and
Historical Theology
Eden Theological Seminary, St. Louis, MO

Praise to Vicars of Tent Town! As I read the book, I felt like Shauna was in my home, sitting by my fireplace telling me these stories in person. You will be quietly wrapped in a cozy blanket of words that will gently inspire and speak to the heart of God. This is a beautiful book about difficult heart issues presented in rare, honest, open and God honoring fashion! You will bear witness to a woman that lives a life as we should. She demonstrates qualities of listening, sharing, hugging, laughing and laying herself before strangers as Jesus did. It is a wonderful inspiration to how we can always improve as Christians to live a little more like Jesus every day. This book speaks to the heart of an amazing story teller about an amazing God and His astounding mission, to fear not and love!

Renee Crosby
Author of *The Fringe: A Secret Society* and
Soup Kitchen for the Soul
Highlands Ranch, CO

Vicar of Tent Town is a different kind of inspirational book. Not preachy, not spoken from a superior perspective, but a simple retelling of the peace that comes from knowing you are where you're supposed to be. Shauna is clearly a woman who is comfortable with the purest, rawest emotions of the human heart, and while she ministers to those, it's also where she finds her solace. No pretense, no artifice - this "Vicar" calmly knows, and reminds us, that there is pain, but ultimately there is God.

Lisa Starcher Collins

Moving, inspiring, and challenging! The stories and deep reflection contained in this book reveal the call and heart of a pastor. The interweaving of personal story and biblical reflection masterfully reveal a passionate challenge to discover and engage God's children who live at the physical and spiritual edges of our communities in every town, city, and in every place. The writer shares a journey of being convicted, taking risks, and discovering the gift of relationships that challenge the reader to begin an individual journey "to step outside their own lives and truly become a part of the life of another." This book is an invitation to sit, eat, and listen; and to choose love and relationship with others over avoidance and judgment. This book calls us to open our eyes, hearts, minds, and spirits to experience something beyond ourselves; and summons us to actions which reveal that "Christ's hands are amongst the living."

Sandra L. Steiner Ball
Resident Bishop, West Virginia Conference
The United Methodist Church

THE VICAR OF TENT TOWN

SHAUNA M. HYDE

Energion Publications
Gonzalez, FL
2015

Cover Design: Henry Neufeld

ISBN10: 1-63199-157-4
ISBN13: 978-1-63199-157-8
Library of Congress Control Number: 2015938150

Energion Publications
P. O. Box 841
Gonzalez, FL 32560
850-525-3916

energion.com
pubs@energion.com

DEDICATION AND PRAYER

This book is lovingly dedicated to those who are brave enough to be the hands, feet, and heart of God in this world with special regard to those who went without question: Jim, Sheri, Fritz, John, Kim, Shirley, the Bistro staff who hold a special place in my heart and all those who give and serve so willingly and lovingly.

To Frank and Tom, true knights in the greatest chess game of all: life!

To social workers, teachers, hospital staff, church staff, and all those who work diligently work to transform this world:

May God hold you gently, give you strength, and inspire you with great love. Amen.

God,
I pray that if my heart must be broken,
it would be broken free of hate, guilt, and selfishness.
If I must be tired, I would be tired of injustice.
If I must lose my way, it would be that I lost myself in You.
If I must fail, I would fail to doubt You.
If I must fall, I would fall on my knees to serve others.
If I must bow under pressure, I would bow in prayer to my God.
If I must err, I would ever and always err on the side of grace. Amen.

Shauna's prayer, 2006

Table of Contents

INTRODUCTION

… since all have sinned and fall short of the glory of God.
– Romans 3:23

Beloved, let us love one another, for love is from God, and whoever loves has been born of God and knows God. Anyone who does not love does not know God, because God is love. – 1 John 4:7-8

See what kind of love the Father has given to us, that we should be called children of God; and so we are. The reason why the world does not know us is that it did not know him. – 1 John 3:1

Being a social justice pastor does not mean that I am to always be in ministry to people on the fringes of society. It doesn't mean that I will always be in a town where there are homeless people or people who are obviously in the Fringe. (Reference to a wonderful book, *The Fringe: A Secret Society* by Renee Crosby.)

People are the same everywhere and in every town and community, there are those who are slightly on the outside of the mainstream of that community. There will always be those people who do not quite fit in, who are not quite accepted, and who seem to struggle to understand cultural norms.

The truth that many of us cannot truly accept is that we are all broken. Not having a bed to sleep in or car to drive does not define someone as broken. The uneasy truth that I have discovered is that some of the most broken people hide in lovely homes, nice clothes, busy schedules, important jobs, and familiar prejudices. They can deny their brokenness and keep on the disguise. What sets people on the fringes apart is that they know and fully own the truth that they are broken. They have nothing to hide behind, no lie to offer to disguise the truth, no possessions and titles to divert unwanted attention.

Sometimes the people who are most on the fringes of faith, forgiveness, pain, and doubt are the people we see every day. We work with them, worship with them, live with them, and play with them. They have bought into the lie and fail to see how broken they are and how much God loves them.

We are taught to hide brokenness because it is shameful and people will talk about us. What people think of us is often more important than anything else so we live the lie and drift further and further into the emotional, mental, and spiritual fringes of life.

We are all broken. We are all precious. We are all dearly loved by God. God dearly desires that we be made whole.

How do we get to the emotional fringe? Humanity is an odd bag of expectations, double standards, and lost dreams. Somewhere woven through it all is the extraordinary ability to love, hope, forgive, and live in peace. We begin to drift toward the Emotional and Spiritual Fringe when we fall prey to judgment and criticism. They are swords that cut both ways – to the victim and to the perpetrator.

The victim begins to bow under the weight of judgment and criticism and slowly the pain turns to bitterness and the anger to a relentless hate. They begin to internalize and the guilt that has been heaped upon them by those who have found them lacking becomes the shame they use to define themselves. Slowly the words, "You are a sinner," become the words, "I am sin." The words, "You are doing that wrong," become the words, "I am what is wrong." Shame drives people to the fringes as surely as a bus can take you to Toledo.

People who let themselves become defined by shame become hard to convince that God does love them and will forgive them.

For the perpetrator, judgment and criticism become attitudes that can be a mask to hide fear and low self-esteem. The longer they hide and the more they find wrong with the world and the people around them, the more isolated they become. The only emotional state they feel comfortable in is judgment and criticism. It becomes what defines them. They become harsh and unforgiving. When a person is on the emotional and spiritual fringe in this manner, they are unable to feel the presence of God and begin to believe that God will not forgive them. Instead of admitting it, they impose that thought onto others. Often how we describe God and view God is really a picture of ourselves.

These are the truly destructive and dangerous fringes in which dwell. These are the fringes we must all guard against. If we could accomplish it, we might make true change in the world and the physical fringe of society would be cared for, those who live there brought into the fold, and those who fear it would love instead.

– Shauna Hyde

Chapter 1

The Beginning

³¹ 'When the Son of Man comes in his glory, and all the angels with him, and then he will sit on the throne of his glory. ³² All the nations will be gathered before him, and he will separate people one from another as a shepherd separates the sheep from the goats, ³³ and he will put the sheep at his right hand and the goats at the left. ³⁴ Then the king will say to those at his right hand, "Come, you that are blessed by my Father, inherit the kingdom prepared for you from the foundation of the world; ³⁵ for I was hungry and you gave me food, I was thirsty and you gave me something to drink, I was a stranger and you welcomed me, ³⁶ I was naked and you gave me clothing, I was sick and you took care of me, I was in prison and you visited me." ³⁷ Then the righteous will answer him, "Lord, when was it that we saw you hungry and gave you food, or thirsty and gave you something to drink? ³⁸ And when was it that we saw you a stranger and welcomed you, or naked and gave you clothing? ³⁹ And when was it that we saw you sick or in prison and visited you?" ⁴⁰ And the king will answer them, "Truly I tell you, just as you did it to one of the least of these who are members of my family, you did it to me." ⁴¹ Then he will say to those at his left hand, "You that are accursed, depart from me into the eternal fire prepared for the devil and his angels; ⁴² for I was hungry and you gave me no food, I was thirsty and you gave me nothing to drink, ⁴³ I was a stranger and you did not welcome me, naked and you did not give

me clothing, sick and in prison and you did not visit me." [44] Then
they also will answer, "Lord, when was it that we saw you hungry
or thirsty or a stranger or naked or sick or in prison, and did not
take care of you?" [45] Then he will answer them, "Truly I tell you,
just as you did not do it to one of the least of these, you did not do
it to me." [46] And these will go away into eternal punishment, but
the righteous into eternal life.'   – Matthew 25:31-46

Charlie

Of the three men who changed my life the most, I met Charlie
first. I had been at the church just a couple of weeks. It was Sunday
morning and I was flitting around doing the one million little tasks
that must be done on Sunday before church. On one of my many
trips up and down the aisle I saw an elderly gentleman drop his
hearing assist. I stopped and knelt down, picked it up, and handed
it to him. As I knelt before him, looking up at him, I noticed his
kind eyes and beautiful smile. He was still handsome and charming
and had me wrapped around his finger within the first five minutes
of our relationship. He kindly thanked me and I continued on my
flitting dash getting ready for the church service. Later, I was told
that he was one of the church members who had insisted it was
time for another female minister and had supported my appointment to that church before I had even arrived. I had no idea what
was in store for me and the great love I would share with this man.
He was to become grandfather, mentor, champion, kindred spirit,
and close friend. I cherish the memory of meeting him to this day.

Robert

I met Robert soon after meeting Charlie. A few weeks into my
arrival at the church I was standing in the narthex of the church
when an energetic flurry of activity announced his arrival. I looked
to the door as a tall, thin, forty-something, Asian man walked in.
He wore what I would soon come to recognize as his regular attire
of a black pants and a black t-shirt with the name of his restaurant

on it. He walked up to me, hugged me right away, and said, "You must be Shauna. We are so excited you are here." He introduced me to his wife, Sherri, and told me of their role in the church as they carted food in for a church function. They were to become partners in ministry and the catalyst for amazing events at the church.

Noah

I had been at the church for a while when I started hearing stories about the people who lived in tents by the river. The location of the church is in downtown Charleston, WV, and is close to many of the mission houses, ministries, and shelters for the homeless and indigent population in the area. One of my primary roles at the church was to manage the assistance ministries in which we helped to pay bills, referred to the shelters, and gave out bus tokens, clothing, diapers, blankets, etc. I had quickly become fairly familiar with many of the regulars and had enough of a relationship with some of them that I believed them. After hearing, yet again, about the folks on the river, I went to my office and started to put some of the stories together. As I was trying to piece the stories together to get an approximate location and number of people, I looked up and found myself looking into the eyes of Jesus. I had a large painting of Jesus in my office and when I was sitting at my desk I was at eye level with Jesus. As I looked at that picture I knew what I needed to do, so I grabbed my keys, changed my shoes, and headed off to the river. I parked and hiked around a bit and finally found the trail. As I followed the trail and came down the hill to the camp, I hollered, "Ho, the camp." A couple of men came out and watched me come down the hill. All around me was an assortment of tents in various states of disrepair, old chairs, blankets, and a fire pit dug and built into the ground. The men were joined by others and I entered the camp. I introduced myself and told them I was from the church downtown, had heard about them, and was there to check on them. They invited me to sit and began to introduce themselves (first names only). We chatted a bit about their camp, the weather, and what they needed. I told them I would return with the list of supplies they had requested. I asked who would be there upon my return and one man stepped forward. He was thin, fairly tall, and had a long drooping mustache. His name was Noah and Noah was going to change my life forever.

CHAPTER 2

SONGS

He has told you, O mortal, what is good; and what does the Lord require of you
but to do justice, and to love kindness, and to walk humbly with your God? — Micah 6:8

Charlie

The time came around when the new church directory needed to be made. A church member and I were to go around to all the shut-ins, homebound, special needs members and take their picture for the directory. Charlie was on the list of people whose picture we were to take. We went to his home and found him waiting for us. He asked if we could take his picture with him holding the picture of his wife. As we took pictures he told us about his wife who had already passed away. His love and devotion to her was still evident. As he told us of the places they had been and the life they had, he asked me if I would do him a favor. He took me over to the baby grand piano and pulled out a sheet of music and asked me if I could and would play it for him. I sat down and started to play it and when I looked up at him I saw tears running down his cheeks. The song had been one of *their* songs and was still a favorite. He told me of the moment when they heard it for the first time on a trip, behind the then Iron Curtain, by a pianist in a restaurant lobby and how he hunted until he found the music for it! He shared of the countless times they played it for each other. The name of that song for me will forever be, "Jean's Song." You may have heard it called *Ballade Pour Adeline*. There would never be another visit to Charlie's house in which that song would not be played for him. I would play it and look up to find him quietly crying. He would say, "Just one more time, please play it just one more time." I spent hours playing for him. Those are hours of my life I will never regret.

Robert

Robert called me one day and asked me to come to the restaurant as he and Sherri needed to talk to me. Upon my arrival, we sat in a booth sharing some soup and cake and he began to talk, "Shauna, we are just so upset right now about the stance the UMC has taken on homosexuality. I just don't know if we can stay when we are being encouraged to exclude people. A lot of the people we hire are people who are estranged from church – some of them for being gay. We don't like them thinking that the church we go to wouldn't accept them."

I pushed back my plate and thought a minute, "You cannot change something from the outside. The beauty of the UMC is that we agree to disagree and worship together despite differences. Keep on showing your people who you are and who God is."

"What can we do when they are getting the message that the church as a whole is exclusive?"

After discussing it for a while, Robert and Sherri decided that they would make their opinion and beliefs clear to those who worked for them. They also were going to put scripture references in with paychecks. Every reference was one about God's grace and love for humanity. They stayed.

Noah

It started to become habit to stop in Tent Town at least once a week, if not more often. Each time we took something useful: can openers, shoes, blankets, wood, food, etc. I would start down the hill and yell, "Ho, in the camp."

Noah would come out to greet me with a smile on his face and a hug ready for the lady preacher.

We would sit by the fire and talk about life, kids, jobs, people, and the weather. It became a time of rest and laughter.

CHAPTER 3

FOLLOWING JESUS

Jesus said, "Follow me!" We avoided that by making the message into something he never said: "Worship me." Worship of Jesus is rather harmless and risk-free; actually following Jesus changes everything.

— Richard Rohr[1]

Charlie

The gentlemen's Bible study took place every Thursday morning at the church. There were two of them who went to Charlie's house to play chess and eat potato chips after Bible study. One day, I was invited to tag along.

Soon, it became the norm to go to Charlie's house on Thursday afternoons. There would be bowls of potato chips, glasses of Coke, and games of chess accompanied by discussion on theology, philosophy, and politics.

Charlie began to keep a list of questions and topics he wished to discuss with me. He often told me I was too smart for my own good then he would hug me and tell me how pretty I was. It didn't matter how much of a feminist I might be, an 88-year-old man who truly loved me was never reprimanded or brushed off.

1 http://uuawayoflife.blogspot.com/2014/07/thought-for-day-follow-me-or-worship-me.html

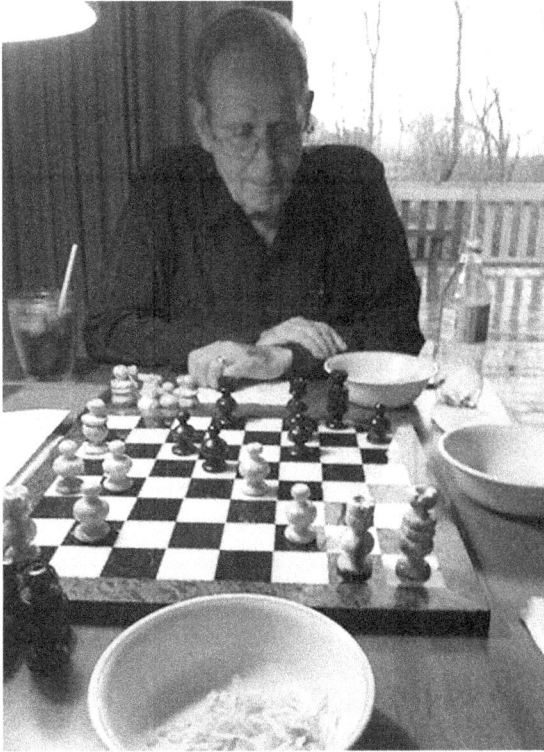

Robert

One day, I received another phone call from Robert asking me to again stop by the restaurant for lunch. We sat in a booth again sharing soup and cake. This time he had a specific plan in mind. He wanted to feed people who needed to be fed. He wanted to touch the lives of those who went to bed with no dinner or had to go the weekend without much food. He wanted to work in conjunction with the other agencies that provided meals and asked me to look into a way we could help and not compete.

Our partnership began as I took his idea to the church staff and to the various committees that needed to approve it. We began to nail down details and work out how we could do this long-term. Robert said, "If we start this, we have to keep it going. Once we have earned people's trust, we cannot stop."

I said, "OK! Let's set it up for the long haul."

The church staff and committees said, "OK! Let's set it up for the long haul!"

Noah

As I did more and more work in the community and in the church, Tent Town became a place of refuge for me. Noah calmly accepted me with my flurry and hurry and would simply clear off a spot on the old used broken- down camp chairs. We would sit and watch the river. If I fell asleep, He would stand guard, keeping me covered and the fire burning. He never complained.

CHAPTER 4

TENT TOWN

I had seen Barbara every day since my arrival in Charleston. She always walked the same route pushing her buggy. One day, I stopped and introduced myself. I began to meet her for lunch at one of the local free meal places. We talked about life and family. She asked me questions about God: "Does God love me?" "Why do Christians treat me so badly if God loves me?" "Why do people blame me for being the way I am?"

After several months of meeting and talking, she asked me for my business card. After I gave it to her, she taped it to her buggy. She looked at me and said, "I want people to know who to call for my funeral when the time comes. I want a preacher there who actually knows me."

"There are people in the world who are so hungry that God would not dare come in any form other than food."

– M. Ghandi

Charlie

Charlie and I began to stay and talk after the others had left the chess game. We began to work through his list. After talking for a while, he would inevitably go to the baby grand he had in the corner of the room and ask me to play his song.

There would be the chess board with the pieces still as we left them from the ongoing game. The smell of chips would be in the air and the ice in our glasses would be completely melted. As silence descended, Charlie would look up and ask something like,

"So what do you believe is God's nature?"

"Do you think all religions actually worship the same God?"

"What do you think it means to have free will?"

We never lacked for anything to talk about. We shared pictures of family and the exploits of our children. He shared memories of Jean and mourned her loss every day. One day he looked at me and asked, "Why do you think we have to get old and suffer?"

I took his hand and asked him, "Why do you think we get old and suffer?"

He sighed and replied, "I am often not sure. I know God loves me but I think we hurt too much."

"Charlie, is God's love for us supposed to keep us from being hurt or feeling any pain?"

"Well, I guess that doesn't make much sense, does it?"

"Not really. Somewhere between toddler and big kid age, our kisses quit making skinned knees all better."

"Do you believe God kisses us?"

"Yes, I do. There is a kiss with every skinned knee, every cancer diagnosis, every broken heart, every time we fail. I just think that somewhere between being a toddler and being a big kid we stop feeling it or believing that God's love really is enough."

"Do you really believe God's love is enough for us?"

"Charlie, if it wasn't, then why has God invested so much love into us?"

Charlie laughed softly and said, "That's a good point. Maybe I just need to skin my knee again."

We laughed and refilled our bowls with potato chips.

Robert

Robert and I met a few more times to work out all the details for the free meal. He set the date and time to begin, decided the financial information, contacted all the other shelters and ministries in the area, handed out flyers, recruited people to cook, serve, clean, act as hosts, and all the multitude of decisions that must be made. We nearly always split a piece of cake.

Feeding people was his passion. Showing people God's love was his goal. Robert had the unique ability to love everyone regardless of social standing. He did not buy into the materialism and consumerism of today's society. He believed in second and third and fiftieth chances and gave them repeatedly. Free dinner on Wednesday evenings was another third chance that was going to be offered to many people.

Noah

One day, I started taking congregation members with me to Tent Town. We would sit and talk and laugh. When we left, I would always hear, "They are just like us!" It always surprised people to realize that the people who lived in Tent Town were normal people with jobs, families, broken dreams, colds, and stories to tell – just like us.

There's a song that keeps me grounded through all my experiences, "The Story" by Brandi Carlile. You can find the lyrics and listen to the music on a number of web sites.[1]

---

1   Lyrics only: http://www.azlyrics.com/lyrics/brandicarlile/thestory.html (last accessed 04/09/15). Lyrics and music: https://play.google.com/music/preview/Ta3hlbiknhjlrddqcbracpkdooy?lyrics=1 (last accessed 04/09/15).

CHAPTER 5

TENT TOWN REVISITED

Billy Jo came to show me every day the coin he earned in AA for being sober for 30 days. The problem was that he was drunk every day he showed it to me. Finally one day I asked him why the coin meant so much to him. He replied that it meant that he might be able to get sober again. I asked him if he was going to try. He said, "Maybe, one day."

He continued to show it to me every day. Every few months we would have the same conversation and then he would continue to remain in a state of drunkenness.

One day he showed up sober. He asked, "Do you notice anything different about me?"

"You're not drunk."

He said, "I realized I could still change."

"What made you able to know that?"

"Well," he said, "I began believing that God *could* love me and forgive me."

"What made you change your mind?"

"Every day I saw God in your eyes."

CHAPTER 6

ESSAY ON "THOSE PEOPLE"

People in poverty become labels and statistics a in way that almost makes them invisible to the rest of society. I have heard over and over again that I should be afraid "going in there" and that they are just "lazy" and that "if they would just get a job …" Let's talk about that for a minute.

You see, it is simply not that clear cut. Did you know that most homeless people are our veterans? Yes, it's true. They come home to find life as they knew it is gone, changed, and that it went on without them. They come home to broken families, no jobs, and are often suffering from PTSD (Post Traumatic Stress Disorder). They have changed. Many have been injured physically, mentally, emotionally, and spiritually. Too many find that they simply have nowhere to go.

Did you know that another large percentage of homeless people are homosexual kids who were kicked out of their homes? The *fortunate* ones do not end up in the sex trade just to survive.

We really need to be careful when we talk about "those people." Many people who live in poverty do have jobs. The problem is that a lot of jobs are at places that only pay minimum wage, do not give 40 hours per week so that benefits do not kick in, and there is no sick pay. Many work more than one job and *still* cannot pay the bills. They learn that it is easier not to work and to receive government funds. We say they have no self-respect; they say they are tired of losing.

People say, "Well, they should quit wasting their money." We say that because if they have a cell phone and cable TV they are wasting money. If they are, are we *not* wasting money simply because we *can* afford it? TV is a stress-reliever and a phone is needed to call for jobs, to call the babysitter, and to call the schools where their children are.

You see, poverty is a culture that is different than middle-class culture or wealthy culture. People who live in poverty are in survival mode. They live from day to day. Their priorities are to survive one day at a time and maintain relationships at all costs (including what the middle class calls 'drama'). Middle-class culture has priorities that include gaining security, gaining possessions, and getting ahead. Wealthy culture has priorities that include being remembered, leaving a legacy, and sustaining their wealth. Do you see how different each one is? We keep trying to impose middle class standards on people whose priorities are survival based. It simply does not work.

We get angry that the lady who needs help paying her electric bill has a Gucci bag, a great nail job, and a cell phone. Stop a minute. In her world, the sexiest and the strongest survive. She also lives day to day. It is an extreme luxury to plan for tomorrow so when she gets the money to look good and stay sexy so a man will choose her instead of someone else, guess what her choice is? For her, it is the only possible choice. The phone may be government provided but she needs it to call her case worker and to make all the same important phone calls we make. Her Gucci bag may very well have come from the Goodwill so don't judge.

There is always a great deal of drama associated with people in poverty because of their priority of maintaining relationships. Remember the strongest and the sexiest survive. To the middle class their language and behavior is vulgar, crude, and impolite. To them, being polite in a struggle to survive would make them appear weak. If they are weak, they will not be selected as a partner, they might be bullied and stolen from, and they are the last to get any favors or extras.

Relationships are important because to be alone is to be weak, unprotected, and preyed upon. A team, a unit, a family is always built regardless of how inappropriate it may be deemed by others from other cultures. They take care of each other. Their family situations, teams, and units are often in flux as dramas play out and the strongest and sexiest are identified and the leaders of the family emerge.

There is no saving, planning for tomorrow, or paying the bill that is due next week because tomorrow may not come, more money may not come, and the goal is to get through today.

We have to stop imposing the cultural norms on them that do not apply. We have to stop expecting everyone to be like us or to force them to be like us. We have to start accepting people as they are, being with them in this moment and in this place.

Chapter 7

The Character of God

Charlie

Charlie was waiting one day with his list of questions in hand. After we got our chips and Coke, he asked, "What is the nature of God?"

"Charlie, you know the minute we answer that question, we will be wrong!"

"What do you mean?"

"Well, we each experience God differently at different times in our lives so each of us would describe God differently. I guess the key is to never assume we have fully described God. There will always be more."

"Ah, yes........God created us in God's image and we keep trying to return the favor."

We sat and munched a few minutes. Then he asked, "What is the point of going to heaven?"

"What do you think the point is?"

"Well, I just really want to see Jean again."

"Charlie, heaven is being fully in the presence of God with no barriers any more. We have been assured there will be a reunion but the whole purpose of heaven is to finally be fully free of all barriers and to be with God."

"I never thought of it that way. So, what would you say Hell is?"

"I always thought of Hell as the place where we go when we have fully rejected and turned away from the presence of God with a hatred so intense that we do incredibly cruel things in this world."

"So, what about those who are angry with God and reject God?"

"I think there is a special place in God's heart for those who have been deeply hurt, are suffering, are lost, and are angry. There is a big difference between rejecting due to anger and hurt and being able to heal, and rejection due to hatred so intense that healing cannot be achieved. Hell could also be apathy or ...."

The afternoon passed by in a whirlwind of descriptions and "what if's." The nature of God, of humanity, the history of the Bible, and other topics were bantered about, discussed, and books were referred to as ideas were looked up and scriptures were checked.

The smell of salt and the soft popping of Coke in a glass filled the air as we flipped pages and asked each other questions.

CHAPTER 8

ANOTHER EVENING IN
TENT TOWN

I met Adam one day when I went to visit Tent Town. He was dark and handsome and quiet. He spoke softly and struggled with addiction. He had lost everything and was working on getting through each day as best as he could. He desperately needed to be reassured that God would forgive him. He believed he was too horrible and had done too many terrible things for God to forgive him.

We sat on the ground close to the fire in Tent Town. Adam was shivering with cold and withdrawal. "Preacher, God really will forgive anyone who asks to be forgiven?"

"Yes, Adam, God does not withhold forgiveness. To do so would make what Jesus did for us a moot point."

"But, I am such a bad person."

"You are a human being worthy of love and forgiveness. Don't give up on yourself. God doesn't give up on you."

Tears rolled down his cheeks as he jammed his hands deeper into his jacket pockets.

"I wish I could believe you. I really do." He looked so miserable, so bleak and hopeless that it broke my heart.

We just sat for a while and watched the fire.

Chapter 9

The Parable of the Good Samaritan

^{25} Just then a lawyer stood up to test Jesus. 'Teacher,' he said, 'what must I do to inherit eternal life?' ^{26} He said to him, 'What is written in the law? What do you read there?' ^{27} He answered, 'You shall love the Lord your God with all your heart, and with all your soul, and with all your strength, and with all your mind; and your neighbor as yourself.' ^{28} And he said to him, 'You have given the right answer; do this, and you will live.'

^{29} But wanting to justify himself, he asked Jesus, 'And who is my neighbor?' ^{30} Jesus replied, 'A man was going down from Jerusalem to Jericho, and fell into the hands of robbers, who stripped him, beat him, and went away, leaving him half dead. ^{31} Now by chance a priest was going down that road; and when he saw him, he passed by on the other side. ^{32} So likewise a Levite, when he came to the place and saw him, passed by on the other side. ^{33} But a Samaritan while traveling came near him; and when he saw him, he was moved with pity. ^{34} He went to him and bandaged his wounds, having poured oil and wine on them. Then he put him on his own animal, brought him to an inn, and took care of him. ^{35} The next day he took out two denarii, gave them to the innkeeper, and said, "Take care of him; and when I come back, I will repay you whatever more you spend." ^{36} Which of these three, do you think, was a neighbor to the man who fell into the hands *of the robbers?'* [37] *He said, 'The one who showed him mercy.' Jesus said to him, 'Go and do likewise.'*

– Luke 10:25-37

Wade

Wade is a funny little guy. He carries around a bag of blankets and has a long and detailed explanation as to why he carries it. He walks around town bumming cigarettes off people and talking either to himself or to the companions that only he can see. He has a favorite hole in a local park where he likes to sleep at night. The local shelters are nearly always full and on nights when the weather is really bitter they will do their best to get as many people as possible housed in as many places as possible. One night, it was snowing and the temperature was dropping. Wade had not been seen by any of the usual helpers. I was starting to get a bit worried as he usually stuck to his schedule. I bundled up and headed towards the park. I poked around every hole, nook, and cranny and finally found Wade trying to get warm. He was having an especially difficult day and was incoherent as he conversed with his companions. After much ado, he was safely dropped off at the shelter.

I have lost count of the number of times different people have gone out looking for our street family members. Those of us who work with people become familiar with each other's routines and favorite hangouts. We are the ones who write letters home, fill out the applications for them to get birth certificates, and use our addresses at the churches, shelters, and mission houses so they can receive mail. Many of our street family members have a difficult time obtaining information, ID cards, and all the paperwork that validates their existence in today's society. We spend hours at the court house looking up information, trying to find the name of their mother or their birth date because they have forgotten or simply lost that information as their life knowledge became based on what they needed to know for a day to day existence.

Charlie

The day I finally beat Charlie at a game of chess was the day he rewarded me by letting me drive his red Corvette. That was a great day! He sat in the passenger seat and let me tool through town. I was trying so hard to be good and not hurt the car! He finally looked over at me and asked, "Are you going to lay rubber or what?" Needless to say, we laid rubber all over town! Charlie would laugh and absorb each moment. The joy that a car ride gave him was tremendous! I learned to live in the moment and appreciate the joy there.

Robert

Finally we were ready to go!!! All the plans we made. All the necessary approvals gained. All the volunteers recruited. The date and time set and we were a go!!!

Robert came into the church with a big smile on his face and huge containers of food ready to be served. The Fellowship Hall was set up and the hosts were in place. They came! People came into the church to be met with smiles and shown where to go get dinner. People greeted Robert and he learned their names and spent time talking to them. Church members sat and made friends. Week and after week went by with food, laughter, prayers, and friendships formed. We began to know people by name and hear their stories. We went to Tent Town and brought them in to dinner. When winter came and we learned that many were cold and the shelters full, over 150 sleeping bags were distributed. We gave out tarps and tents, socks and shoes, and gave permission to them to sleep in the courtyard of the church where it was protected and warm.

There were more than a few snowstorms in which I and some church members would be combing the streets looking for who we knew might be there and getting them somewhere safe.

Robert had made a family.

Noah

One day when I went into Tent Town, some new people were mixed in with the usual group. As we sat and talked, one of them said, "Hey you look like that lady on *The Vicar of Dibley*!" Everyone started laughing and agreed that I did resemble the character in appearance and in personality. Another of the guys, one of the regulars, said, "We'll just call you the Vicar or Vic!" That was the day the Vicar of Tent Town was named.

We stoked up the fire and started cooking the food I had brought. Several of them worked in local restaurants and knew how to fix a great meal. We cracked open some beer and toasted each other and ate together. When I left I did a tent blessing ceremony on every tent and they smiled, daring to hope that maybe – just maybe – God did care.

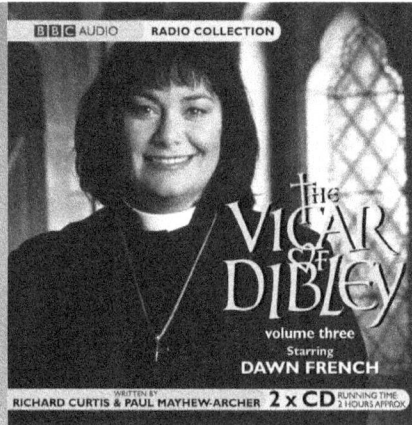

Chapter 10

Broken Hearts

"We have had it wrong for many years in that we have insisted upon being Christian first and then friend. To truly be like Jesus, we must be friend first."

– Bishop William Boyd Grove

I arrived at the camp to find Adam passed out on the road at the top of the hill. I lifted him as best as I could and started to carry/drag him down the hill to his tent. He mumbled, "Vic, do you think God can ever love me?"

"God does love you, Adam."

"I am too terrible. God could never love me."

I continued to drag him to his tent. I managed to get him inside and into his sleeping bag. He began to cry, "I just want to be the person I was. I just want to be better."

I held him while he cried, gently rocking him to sleep. "God loves you, Adam."

Many people think that clergy don't behave the same as the rest of humanity. Many think we don't ask the same questions. There are times when regardless of all the training, despite all the faith and knowing, even when assured of our God and God's goodness, we still ask, "Why, God, why?"

Can we watch one more broken heart weep, one more broken soul cry out for mercy, and one more tragedy unfold? Then God says, "I am here, hold my hand, let **ME** mend the hearts, forgive the souls, and heal the world.... one tragedy at a time..."

So while God holds one hand, we reach out with the other.

CHAPTER 11

REV. BADASS

I have a cigarette taped on the corner of a picture frame in my office. When I get lost in the sea of administration, complaints, problems, and details that clergy often face, I will stop and look at that cigarette. It is a reminder of love, hope, and grace for me. Why?

I was appointed to an urban church located in the midst of the "street community." The street community was a people who were homeless, mentally ill, housed but lonely and *poorly* housed, etc. Many of the organizations that offered assistance were located around the church and the church did a fair portion of the work as well. There was one gentleman associated with the church who struggled through every day. He was a paranoid schizophrenic and had been self-medicating for many years with alcohol. Most of the time he was some level of drunk. He hated the ways the meds made him feel and he had drunk for so long that that was all he knew.

I first met him when he wandered into the church and was telling me his latest conspiracy theory. I soon discovered that all I had to do was listen for a bit and he would wander on. His theories were always interesting. Bit by bit I was allowed to see glimpses of who he had been and what his life was like now.

One day, I was in the sanctuary playing the piano and I noticed someone sitting in the back. I continued to play and they continued to sit. When I was finished, I started to get up and leave when I heard a familiar voice say, "Please continue playing. It has been a long time since I felt such peace." So, I played a while longer. Soon, it became the norm to see him sitting in the sanctuary anytime I was playing. Sometimes if he came into the church and was agitated, I would just take him into the sanctuary and would start to play and he would become calm again. After about one year, he began to make requests so I began learning new music just because he had asked for it.

It has been my practice at every appointment to send out birthday cards or letters. One year I sent him a birthday letter. He came to see me the day he received it. His eyes were filled with tears and he was trembling with emotion as he quietly thanked me for what he felt was a tremendous gift. He had nothing to give me but he wanted to give me something in return. So, he reached into his pocket and emptied it out. There were a couple of pennies, some lint, and a broken cigarette. He gave me the broken cigarette, a shaky hug, and many tears of gratitude.

I have kept that cigarette to remind me not to get so caught up in the machine that I forget to see the people. Every time I see that cigarette and think of him, I am reminded that it does not take much to connect with someone and to offer them something valuable. That broken cigarette is a precious reminder that many of us are simply not yet able to be what others think we should be. Some of us struggle through life with such horrible burdens that a letter, a little music, and a cigarette mean more than any amount of money, time, gifts, or extravagance ever could. I do not believe I am truly capable of putting into words how much that broken cigarette means to me. When I get discouraged, tired, and wonder if I am doing any good at all, that cigarette reminds me to focus on one person at a time. The to-do list will always be there while the trust and love of a suffering soul has to be earned. The problems will always be there in one form or another while music must be played in order for a soul to find peace. So, I see the cigarette and I go play the piano. I see the cigarette and I stop to pray for someone, call someone, write a note to someone, or go see someone. That broken cigarette is precious to me because it is an example of trust and love being freely given by someone so broken it was all they had to give. What is your cigarette?

Chapter 12

Learning to Love: First Time at West Virginia Day of Fairness

When writing about what it was like to be at the Capitol building for the West Virginia Day of Fairness in February (2014), I had to think about it for a while because I wasn't sure how to express how I felt and what I saw that day. I, like many clergy, often try to avoid uncomfortable situations or being some place that our congregation would question or be upset about. Going to the Capitol that day actually made me a bit anxious because I did not know what to expect. What would people think? How would people react to a woman running around in a clerical collar with LGBTQ people demanding to be treated fairly?

Well, I got to where I was supposed to be and was greeted with warm hugs and happy smiles. A variety of people showed up and I saw that they had a bit of an anxious look about them too. I came prepared, though, for a clerical collar possibly causing discomfort. I had made silly little valentines cards for everyone, it being close to Valentine's Day — a reminder that, regardless of who we are or how different we might be, we are worthy of being loved and treated well.

As most conferences and events go, there was the usual shuffling about of people and time-frames but everyone jumped in with a smile. As I co-presented, I was able to interact with people who had amazing stories and lived unusual, yet loving, lives.

I have to admit, it can still surprise me to see a transgender person (in this case, a transgender woman) and I found myself focusing on their make-up or their hands with painted nails. But then, something happened. I looked her in the eyes. I saw her – really saw her. I lost sight of the appearance and forgot stereotypes and gender expectations and just saw her. The rest of the day was dramatically changed for me. I was able to look each person in the eye and hear their story. Their stories involved all manner of partnerships and family groupings. Their stories involved some heartache and some joy. They all involved love. I heard love story after love story. I saw family after family and I quit being worried about what anyone would think.

I told stupid jokes and silly stories to get our minds off the cold and the shuffling around. They figured out quickly that I was just a goof! But they had looked into my eyes and had seen me too, so it was okay.

The bottom line for me, standing with people who demand to be treated fairly, is that within our scriptures and within our social principles we have determined that all people have the right to homes, jobs, and to be treated well. Too many people never look past the differences and learn to love. I am reminded of the line in *Les Miserables* that says, "To love another is to touch the face of God." Each time I am with LGBTQ people, I am thankful because I have been taught how to love and how to be loved in a deeper and more meaningful way than I ever dreamed.

CHAPTER 13

ANOTHER ESSAY ON "THOSE PEOPLE"

Why do people choose to live outside instead of in the shelters or getting a home?

Shelters, while well monitored, are often places of violence and theft. What precious little someone may own often disappears in a shelter. Remember their culture is based on survival so in a shelter there is a distinct pecking order. Many people just get tired of it and want a life of peace.

Living in shelters also comes with a lot of strict rules. People must be in by a certain time of night or they do not get a bed. They must also be out by a certain time in the morning. At some, you must have a job so if someone gets sick, gets fired, or cannot get a job they have no bed that night.

Many shelters also require that the people attend church services and many people are not interested because to them God has left and does not really care about them or they would not be where they are.

Many veterans do not want to be in one more building that might blow up and where they might be attacked. They suffer from such tremendous PTSD they cannot bear to be anywhere but in the open air.

Shelters also often split up families and couples due to space or lack of proof that they are married, etc. This is unsettling and for them it places them in a weak position because their unit/team/ family has been split up.

So, they find a place to sleep outside. They find cubbies in sidewalks, holes in parks, dents in buildings, and spaces under bridges where it is warmer and the weather doesn't keep them from sleeping.

Many of them have college degrees and are highly intelligent. Most of them have had a series of life events that really could happen to any one of us. We just do not want to admit it because we are too scared to think of it.

Some of them just do not buy into society. They look at our lives and think we are crazy. We work long days for other people. We work to pay bills that really are not necessary. We have to leave our families even when the weather is bad. Most of us live with a great deal of stress. They have simply asked the question, "Who said they were right?" They refuse to live as we do.

Chapter 14

Change in Thinking

Charlie

One Thursday I was over at Charlie's house and he knew that I was deeply troubled by something. It wasn't often that I lost to him anymore – not with a red Corvette ride as a prize!

I had not talked to anyone yet and was unsure of what to tell, and who to tell which part about what had occurred. Charlie asked and waited quietly for me to open up.

I finally said, "Last night, my son came home and said he needed to talk to me. I was washing the window in the door and just told him I was listening. He was quiet for a minute and then he said, 'Mom, I'm gay.' I just remember thinking that I didn't know what to do and that he was going to be hurt and rejected in this life and that I could never tell anyone because they would hate him and judge him. I just kept washing the door because I didn't know how to handle what he said but I knew how to wash that door. I prayed for God to show me what to do and when I turned around I didn't see an adult son, I saw him at three-years-old when he had been hurt and scared and just wanted his mom. I knew then that he was hurt and scared and just wanted his mom. I simply said, "OK." He cried and I cried and we knew that we could face whatever we had to face together."

Charlie was quiet for a minute and then said, "How do you feel about it today?"

"Today, I am scared because I do not know what to expect. I was raised one way – conservative and fundamental. I went to seminary and learned another way. I learned how we interpret the scriptures differently than intended and that there is much that we have not represented well. I know that this fight is something that has troubled me for many years and I have had too many questions that people cannot answer well. I have learned that this is not about an issue, it is about people and God loves people."

"What are you going to do with your son?"

"I am going to love him, Charlie. I am going to stand by him and walk with him through this life. I have prayed for him and taught him as best as I can. Being gay is not about who he is it is about who he loves. He is smart, talented, funny, and loving. He loves God and is seeking and studying for answers. I am going to love him and be his mom."

Charlie took my hand and said, "That is the best answer you could ever give. The rest doesn't matter, does it?"

I wiped my face and sighed, "Well, I know this, Charlie: I know that Christians believe we are saved by the death and resurrection of Jesus Christ. Our salvation is based on the blood of Christ not on our sexuality. He is a Christian with a deep commitment to and faith in God. We will take it one day at a time."

Over the next few months a story about me broke in the local newspaper. People were either supportive of a minister with a gay son or they were extremely hate-filled. Charlie helped me burn the hate mail that came to my door. He held me while I cried over people saying my son was going to Hell and me with him. He held my hand as I struggled to be a Christian minister when Christians turned on the hate and went after us with everything they had.

The church I served stood fast and solid, loving us and holding us just as Charlie loved and held me during the long months of fear and adjustment, and as life, family, and friends reacted to the news and life as we knew it changed forever.

Chapter 15

A New Community

It is difficult to put into words all that happened and exactly how I felt. There is so much conflict around the issue of homosexuality that most people try to avoid it or have adamantly made up their minds and that is that. I had to take a different tack and approach it head on with conversation, prayer, study, and letting myself be open to multiple possibilities and answers.

The hardest part was receiving hate mail and even death threats from people who called themselves Christian. The irony is that the very people that were hated and viewed as evil by those Christians were the ones who reached out to me and my son and simply loved us. They surrounded us and supported us and built a wall of comfort around us that was impenetrable. The church I served was loving and the complete antithesis of those who would send notes. I had to reframe my definition of Christians, love, acceptance, and evil, recognizing that at the root of the issue is great fear.

I was able to put away hate and angst when I focused on the great depth that drives someone to write such horrible comments and send it anonymously. If they have to admit that how they interpret the Bible, how they believe, what they think, what they have built their life and salvation on is different than how they thought a real fear takes root because even if they are not fully aware of it, they are questioning the truth of their own salvation and redemption. If they are "wrong" about one thing, what else might they be "wrong" about? Fear is what drives hate. We must settle our own soul before God, so that we can love others without the overwhelming need to make them be like us so that we can be affirmed.

I began a ministry in and with many people who are in the LGBTQ community and I discovered such heartbreak that it will be a long time before I recover.

People have killed people for being gay. People have taunted, tormented, and abused people who are gay. Fear drives hate.

I met a young man who had suffered greatly at the hands of others for being gay. He had endured brain washing techniques in an attempt to be fixed. He had suffered through electric shock treatments. It had all been against his wishes. When he met me I was wearing my clerical collar and was there in an official capacity. He recoiled from me in fear and hid behind the other people there. I shook his hand and smiled. Later, he relaxed enough to enter into conversation with me. At the end of our conversation, during which we both shed many tears, I hugged him and started to leave.

He looked at me with tears in his eyes and said, "No one with Reverend in front of their name has ever hugged me."

I left broken-hearted. Where would Jesus be today?

CHAPTER 16

WHAT THE FAMILY GOES THROUGH

We treat people badly in this world. Anyone who is different from what has been deemed "normal" by society has a hard time in life. We have seen many news stories of LGBTQ people being bullied, tortured, and killed. We have seen bullying of those who are mentally and physically handicapped. We have seen those who are mentally ill be bullied and stereotyped. It is an endless list of anyone we feel justified in being against. It could be prostitutes, addicts, Muslims, red-necks, hillbillies, Christians, Baptists, and the list goes on. If we feel justified in being against them and treating them badly nothing and no one stops us. We often forget the families of those we deem worthy of horrific treatment.

The grief that a family goes through when someone comes out is not to be minimized, set aside, or picked on. Even when we opt for love and acceptance, there is a grief cycle that must be worked through. We grieve the loss of the identity that we had in our minds of who our relative was. We have to learn to embrace who they *really* are and let go of who we *thought* they were. We mourn the loss of the future we thought was going to happen. We spent years thinking of marriage, children, grandchildren all happening in the "acceptable" ways. Suddenly, we mourn the loss of grandchildren we may never have and the future we thought was going to happen *our* way. We learn to accept other alternative futures and to let go of what we wanted to happen.

I had to accept that there may never be little miniature versions of my son in my future. I have instead embraced the idea that my grandchildren may be adopted, may have surrogate mothers, and may happen in other ways that I was not originally planning on.

We watch for all the little signs that give people away when they realize that our children are different. We are always on edge, ready to protect and defend if needed, and choose close friends with extreme care.

We worry about how they may be hurt and what their future might be like – will they be able to get a job, will they be bullied, will they be beat up and terrorized, etc.? We finally learn to place them in the arms of God and love all the little moments we get that make us smile and slowly trust people again.

To some people they are the gay guy that lives in Apartment #10, the girl at the school with Down's Syndrome, the homeless guy at the street corner, and the lady that wraps her hair up weird like they do in those Arabic countries. To us, they are son, daughter, uncle, brother, father, sister, and precious. Please don't harm them. Remember us.

CHAPTER 17

A FRIEND — A LEGACY

Robert

I was sitting in the church when I received a phone call from Sherri. "Get to the hospital now! Something has happened to Robert!" I went into action notifying those who needed to be notified, taking care of family, church, and details.

Robert died leaving behind hundreds of mourners and a devastated family. I spent hours with his family and with his employees and listened as they told me how he had kept one man's job for him while he did jail time. Robert had kept in contact with him and encouraged him during his sentence. Another employee told about how they could not get a job anywhere due to a record but Robert had given him a chance. They told of how Robert had been part of their lives, keeping them steady, holding them up, and accepting them when no one else would.

The funeral was attended by hundreds of people. All five of the clergy plus the bishop were part of his service. I got to tell how Robert has given me a nickname. Robert loved that I was in the martial arts. He was thrilled when he found out that we actually fought and hit each other. He wanted to know if I had ever had a broken nose or a black eye. He loved it so much that he called me his, "Reverend BadAss." Hundreds of people laughed that day, remembering a man who loved life and had lived life well.

The homeless came dressed in suits and cleaned up. They came not to attend but to tend to those who did. They worked as ushers and helped people find seats, bathrooms, and glasses of water. They came to honor the man who knew their names.

The week after Robert's death we had a memorial service at the community free meal. We opened up the mics for anyone and everyone to talk and to share. Many stood up and bore witness to Robert. They talked about how he knew their names, understood their lives, and never treated them as less than. They cried and sang. We offered communion and invited all to take part.

One man, Johnny, got in line a bit defiantly not truly believing that he would be welcome. He had been treated badly by so many churches that he had lost hope that he was loved and accepted. He received communion for the first time in his life. He was moved to tears and as he hugged me he said, "Shauna, I don't understand it but I know I have taken something into my body that will change me forever." Johnny became a dear friend. One year later, I attended his funeral too.

Chapter 18

God-Defined Family

Noah

The weather was getting really bad. Not only had there been severely cold weather but now it had suddenly heated up and all the ice and snow was melting. People came by the church to tell us that Tent Town was flooding. We jumped in the van and rushed over. We ran up and down the hill getting as much of their meager belongings we could. Finally, we stood at the top of the hill, breathless and cold, watching the last of Tent Town get washed down the river.

The church I served at the time owned a building that was largely empty most of the time. I moved Tent Town into the building as the temperatures dropped to below zero.

The complaints started almost immediately. People in the neighborhood didn't want "those people" living so close to them. They would be doing drugs and stealing and causing problems. The children would not be safe and they would make a mess. I did not make them leave.

The United Methodist Church is run by committees so when it came time for the Trustees to meet again, I had to offer an explanation. It is the responsibility of the trustees to care for the property owned by the church. I pretty much gave them a heart attack when I explained what I had done. Instantly they were concerned with damage, destruction, being sued, etc. (they were doing their job, it's ok!).

The Chairperson asked me if I was asking for their forgiveness. I replied that I was not because I had done nothing wrong. I smiled my prettiest smile and went on to explain that if I were being truly Biblical I would have taken them to my home, not to an empty building. We managed to work out an agreement and the Tent Town people had a place of safety during the harsh weather that followed.

A custodial job came open at the church and I encouraged Noah to apply. A few days later he was employed. He took me to lunch with his first paycheck, smiling as he handed the waiter his bank card to pay for lunch.

When the weather broke we went back to Tent Town and built it again, putting up new tents and cleaning up the mess. They all moved back except for Noah, who now rented a small room in the building from the church.

In the months ahead, Noah would travel with me to other churches and conferences to tell them our story. We remain friends to this day. He is part of my family and is greatly loved.

Chapter 19

Mama

Brenda came and talked with me every Wednesday afternoon before dinner. She called me, "Momma," and would pour out her heart to me. When she needed surgery, she asked me to go with her. When she became pregnant, she asked me if I still loved her.

The ladies at the church had a baby shower for her. She still calls me, "Momma."

When Jesus saw her weeping, and the Jews who came with her also weeping, he was greatly disturbed in spirit and deeply moved. He said, 'Where have you laid him?' They said to him, 'Lord, come and see.' Jesus began to weep. So the Jews said, 'See how he loved him!'   —John 11:33-36

Chapter 20

Another "See You Later!"

Charlie

I received a phone call requesting that I get to the hospital as quickly as possible. When I arrived I found Charlie's family lining the hallway. I recognized the looks on their faces. It was the pinched look of people on the verge of panic and grief. I went into his room and stood by the bedside. He looked so small and frail lying there. A tear ran down his wrinkled cheek as he reached one hand up to me and said, "You are so pretty."

With tears running down my face, I laughed and said, "Are you flirting with me?"

Charlie just laughed. "I have to while I still can."

"Charlie, please don't talk that way. We are not ready to lose you."

He sighed softly and gently stroked my hand. "I just want to go be with Jean. It's time." He pulled me a little closer and, with our foreheads touching, he gave me his blessing. "You will be OK. You are going to change the world. Stay strong and beautiful." We just hugged for a few minutes saying nothing. He held my hand. I cried. His family was talking about making preparations to come home but I knew I would not see him again.

When I finally left for home, I went straight to my piano and sat down. I wanted to play his "Jean's Song" one more time. The music never came. My soul was dry and silent. I was no longer the minister who was to bring comfort. I was just a girl who was losing her best friend. My head fell on the keyboard and I wept with the agony of grief and loss; with the knowledge that I would not see him again.

Charlie died early the next morning. We received the phone call at the church and began to plan the funeral. My soul remained silent.

Charlie died two weeks before my birthday. My birthday was on a Wednesday and when that day arrived I cried most of the day knowing that the following Thursday I would not see Charlie.

There were a lot of Sundays when he would bring me a single yellow rose because "that is what a gentleman does for a lady preacher." On special days, he would bring a single red rose. I knew I would not have a red rose for my birthday. There would be no game of chess, no potato chips, no car ride, and piano music, and no Charlie.

Later that day, I went into the sanctuary to take care of some chores. I noticed something on the altar and went to see what it was. In the center of the altar in a small vase were two yellow roses and a single red rose. The card read, "Happy birthday, Pastor Shauna, from Charlie." I sat down behind the altar and wept the great soul-wracking sobs that bring about healing. As the tears fell, the music slowly began to chime somewhere deep in my soul.

CHAPTER 21

ANOTHER GROUP OF "THOSE PEOPLE"

I have noticed that people tend to treat me differently once they know I have a gay son. I imagine they treat him much differently and even hatefully.

There are some things you need to know:

- Please don't feel sorry for me and express sympathy. My son is not dead. I have not lost him. I may have mourned the loss of the future I anticipated but I have accepted a new normal and the other future he has claimed for himself.

- Please don't tell me he is destined for hell and try to save my soul and his. I can assure you that any Christian parent of a gay child has done more theological, psychological, and scientific research than you will ever do. Do not assume to know what we think, believe, or how we feel.

- Please don't out us. You are not doing us a favor by "preparing" people before we meet them.

- Please don't walk on egg shells around us. We can engage in conversation and be quite all right about the issue. The only difference for us is that instead of it being an issue, it is a person. We have learned how to see past the issue and how to love beyond anyone's beliefs.

- Please don't underestimate the fear we live with. There are so many hate crimes and hate-filled people that we live in terror of what might happen to our child. We pray daily for far more than you might imagine.

- Please don't tell us they can "be fixed." You are working under the assumption they are horrifically broken. First, we are all broken. Work on fixing yourself. Secondly, many of us have researched those programs and have discovered that they do not work and that they tend to be just short of torture in the "treatment" programs.
- Please don't send hate mail. That is cowardly and cruel.
- Please don't tell my son he should kill himself and he and all the other gays are what is wrong with this world. Really?

CHAPTER 22

BROKEN PIECES

Our hearts are broken, our souls shattered. Go ahead: cry, scream, get angry, ask God ,"Why?!" Go ahead: shatter. In the midst of it all remember that God will never leave us or forsake us and God never throws broken pieces away.

— my Facebook post, May 30, 2014

Melissa

I saw her every week at the various free meal places. She was young, pretty, and smiled easily. She wanted a good life. She just hadn't figured out how to stop running yet. She always sought me out to share her week with me. She lived at the shelter, was looking for an apartment, and was taking college classes. As time went by she didn't smile as much or as easily. One day, she came in moving slowly and painfully. Her face was bruised and her smile was gone. I snuck her out the back door away from her boyfriend and we slipped off to the domestic violence shelter. They cared for her there and helped her get her own place and continue her studies. He had knocked several of her teeth out and she did not have the insurance or the help to get her teeth fixed. She rarely smiles now.

CHAPTER 23

DON'T LEAVE

8th Sunday after Pentecost

Matthew 14:13-21

Key Verse: *When it was evening, the disciples came to him and said, 'This is a deserted place, and the hour is now late; send the crowds away so that they may go into the villages and buy food for themselves.' Jesus said to them, 'They need not go away; you give them something to eat.* — Matthew 14:15-16

In the scripture passages preceding Matthew 14, Jesus has been rejected by Nazareth and has received the bad news about the beheading of his cousin, John the Baptist. After he has been given this tragic news, he withdraws wanting to be alone. We can only imagine how he may have felt. At a time of great personal rejection and loss, Jesus has the desire to just be alone; yet a crowd of needy, hungry, seeking people have followed him. Jesus is denied time to pray, meditate, and heal privately, as he must instead turn to people who needed his attention.

So, often in life some tragic event, personal rejection, or bad news leaves us feeling wounded and overwhelmed. We want and need to withdraw and heal, pray, and meditate in a private place. People and circumstances often intervene and we are denied the private time we need.

We must learn to reach out and feed people even when we are wounded, overwhelmed, and hurting. When Jesus reached out instead of sealing himself off from the world a miracle happened. Thousands of lives were touched just as thousands of stomachs were filled.

What are you sealing yourself from today? What hurt are you allowing to prevent you from reaching out and caring for others? Who do you need to feed today? What form do you need to take for someone to see God? Reach out and fill the need. A miracle will happen.

Prayer

God of miracles, thank you being with us when we are rejected, hurting, and overwhelmed. Strengthen us for the work of you kingdom and help us to reach out even when we think we cannot. Amen.

CHAPTER 24

SAVE ME!

9th Sunday after Pentecost

Matthew 14:22-33

Key Verse: *But immediately Jesus spoke to them and said, 'Take heart, it is I; do not be afraid.'*   *– Matthew 14:27*

After Jesus feeds thousands of people, he sends his disciples on ahead of him across the lake. He gets the people to go home and finally he gets an opportunity to be alone to pray and heal and be with God.

The disciples are not experiencing such a peaceful time as a storm has descended upon the lake. Their boat is being tossed around, the waves and wind are battering them as they cling to the boat terrified that death is imminent.

Any of us who have been in a terrifying situation know the desperate prayers that are prayed! We want to be saved! We want the storm to be stopped! We need the assurance that we will be okay! These men surely prayed such desperate prayers.

Yet, when the answer appeared before them; when salvation was standing in front of them, they did not recognize him. How many times have we prayed in desperation for our situation to be changed, for salvation to come and then did not believe God when the answer, the miracle, the salvation is standing before us? When what we were expecting to happen does not happen, we often assume that God did not answer, did not give us what we wanted, said "no," or just did nothing. What form may God have appeared to you and you simply did not recognize him? What forms have you limited God to? What form might God have actually taken? Is God standing before you now, holding the answer to your desperate prayers? Look again. You might be surprised.

Prayer

God of mystery, thank you for hearing our prayers and for responding even when we do not hear, see, or believe. Open our eyes and hearts so that we might better see you. Amen.

CHAPTER 25

SHOUTING

10th Sunday after Pentecost

Matthew 15:(10-20) 21-28

Key verse: *But he did not answer her at all. And his disciples came and urged him, saying, "Send her away, for she keeps shouting after us."* — *Matthew 15:23*

In this story, Jesus and his disciples are just passing through, healing many people on their way. One woman starts shouting at them to get their attention. The disciples start shouting back and then they encourage Jesus to tell her to just go away because she is shouting!

Fortunately, Jesus is wiser and more in touch with human need than his disciples were and he stops to listen. After listening to her, he actually engages in conversation with her and is touched by her great faith.

I have worked a great deal with those in poverty and those who are homeless. There is always a lot of shouting. Shouting at each other, shouting at you (from both those in poverty and to those in the congregation) and often mass chaos and angry confrontations result. People are desperate to be heard, to be acknowledged, and to be affirmed.

The disciples responded as many of us do by wanting to just be rid of her. They did not want to listen, to engage, or to deal with someone who dared to shout at them.

Imagine what miracles would be wrought world-wide if we would just do as Jesus did and stopped to listen. A child was healed and mother was filled with joy simply because Jesus stopped to listen and to engage in conversation instead of simply dismissing her because she was shouting.

Who is shouting around you or at you? Is it loud and vocal or is it silent body-language? Who is desperately trying to be heard, to be acknowledged, and to be affirmed in your life today? Stop and listen. Engage in conversation. A child may be healed, a family restored, hope rediscovered, love found, and God seen by simply stopping to listen.

Prayer

God of many voices, tune our ears and hearts to hearing what is not being said. Fill us with your love and wisdom so that we can answer quietly when others are shouting. Amen.

CHAPTER 26

THOSE PESKY

IMPERFECTIONS

11th Sunday after Pentecost

Matthew 16:13-20

Key Verse: *"And I tell you, you are Peter, and on this rock I will build my church, and the gates of Hades will not prevail against it."*

– Matthew 16:18

This verse is one of the most hope-filled verses in the Bible! Peter was impetuous, often driven by anger, and even denied Christ. He was mouthy and always in trouble. He loved Jesus with his whole being and wanted to do what was right.

Jesus spent a lot of time with him and knew exactly who Peter was and what he would do; yet he told Peter that he was to be a foundation, a rock in the building of God's church.

I tend to be a perfectionist. I can agonize for days and weeks if I think I have done something wrong, not perfect, bad, hurtful, etc. Are you that way too? There is hope for all of us.

Do you hear bad news about churches? Have you heard how a church split or there was a fight? Have you heard about declining membership and all the troubles and travails of churches? There is hope for us.

When Jesus told Peter he would be foundational in building the church, Jesus knew and was deliberately telling Peter and us that he was building that church on our imperfections. We do not have to be perfect. We have been chosen because we are not perfect. Just as God redeems Peter continuously throughout scripture, so God redeems us, our situations, and God's church continuously.

Our job is to become as passion-filled as Peter was so that we will not let our fear of failure and imperfections stop us from being foundational in ministry. What are you afraid of? What is stopping you? Quit it! God is building God's church on you. Step up and be the church for God and for the transformation of this world.

Prayer

God of redemption, help us to put aside our fears, our misgivings, and our excuses so that we may be fully used by you for the building of your church. Amen.

Chapter 27

Association

12th Sunday after Pentecost

Romans 12:9-21

Key verses: *Let love be genuine ...*   *— Romans 12:9a*
... but associate with the lowly.   *— Romans 12: 16b*

Christianity in this century has begun to drastically change for many people and churches. Christians and churches have gotten a bit of a bad reputation due to those among us who are exceedingly critical and judgmental, failing to show love in the process. We have many issues today that seem to be polarizing issues. If you do not know what they are, just watch Facebook for a while. Extreme sides are taken on abortion, medical issues, religious rights, homosexuality, poverty, being on welfare, and the list goes on. For me, it was something that caused a great deal of stress and unhappiness in my life until I went back to the basics.

Jesus ate with sinners, touched lepers, spent time listening to adulterers, prostitutes, and women of ill-repute. He associated with the lowly and ministered to them in love and transformed them and their lives. He tended to "preach" more to the religious folk than he did to those who were unfit, unclean, and horrible.

I have spent a lot of time with all kinds of different people. I didn't used to though because I was always taught that I would be guilty by association and I, as a Christian, should always be above-board. Then something happened. I was so moved by compassion that I looked at a picture of Jesus hanging in my office and could hear him say, "You know where I would be!" I began to go and associate with those who are deemed lowly in today's world. I have been where I was not supposed to go. I went into tent towns, gay bars, drag shows, abortion clinics, pool halls, lottery coffee shops, and on and on. I learned to hear their stories, see their souls, and reach out in love. I learned how to let my love be genuine and to just be with people, forming relationships, slowly and gently changing lives, and simply being God's love with skin on. One day, a drag queen looked at me and said, "I have hated the church for 20 years. After knowing you for three, I am ready to go back to church again." I cried so hard that I think I worried those around us! I loved them. I truly loved them and was loved in return.

Church – God's Church – let our love be genuine. Let our love be more extravagant than our criticism and judgment. Let us dare to be different and to associate with the lowly! Let us not be afraid of what others will think about us or be worried that someone will think we are not Christian. Let us dare to be God's love with skin on!

Prayer

God of love, teach us to love. Open our minds and our hearts so that we may truly see people instead of judging them. Open our arms so that we may reach out, lift up, and hug those who are deemed untouchable. Let your love shine through us with such radiance that the world becomes transformed. Amen.

CHAPTER 28

TESTIMONY

Noah

Noah sat in front of 100 clergy people at a conference and quietly told his story. He spoke about how he ended up homeless and how he felt when a lady preacher, prone to laughing a lot, popped into camp one day. He talked about how we were the only church people who would stay and visit with them. Most people just dumped supplies and left as quickly as possible. He talked about the hardship people in the camp had keeping jobs when they could not get to them, of having to buy certain kinds of clothes to keep a job. He talked about how some struggle with addictions but not all. Most people who struggle with addictions got there by self-medicating mental illness or by trying to minimize some kind of pain, be it physical or emotional. He would know as he had been an intern in a mental hospital for many years.

In his soft voice he answered questions and cracked jokes until they had all fallen in love with him. He cried when he talked about how brave he thought I was just walking into a camp where anyone could have been and sitting down to make friends. Then they started to ask me questions until I cried, talking about how we are called to love in God's name. That means getting dirty, wading through the complicated, and fearlessly walking into a place where the last, the least, and the lost have gathered. It means with-holding judgment and criticism and simply offering more than they expected. It means lifting up instead of putting down. It means choosing love instead of fear-filled hate. Noah received a standing ovation. People hugged him with tears in their eyes as they realized the gift they had been given. Redemption.

CHAPTER 29

OUR MISSION

Robert's and Charlie's graves are on the same hill. I can go and talk to them both, and within my line of sight is the bell tower of the church. Under that tower are homeless people gathering for a meal and God's people gathering to transform the world.

One Sunday morning, a clean shaven well-dressed man approached me and said, "Hello, you probably don't remember me. I used to sit with you around the fire at the camp. I have my own place now. I've been sober for six months. I am coming to church because of the people here. They really love God and let me know that God loved me. I came to thank you for the third chance."

Everywhere in the church people have simply become incorporated into the family. They help serve meals and set up for rummage sales. They are known by name and are hugged. They are part of the Body of Christ.

Chapter 30

Entitlement

I laugh every time I hear someone talk about how the poor and those on welfare have a sense of entitlement. I get pangs in my stomach when I hear people talk about how "those people" are – lazy, spoiled, reliant upon the government system, less than.........

I hear people talk about those who feel entitled with disdain and then I watch the same people get angry about the right of way in traffic, the speed with which someone else is driving, or the parking spot they thought they should have. I hear people insist that they should be treated a certain way and demand respect and courteous treatment and then turn around and treat their wait staff, janitors, and other service personnel with rude contempt.

I observe how people love to talk about "those people" and get offended at the sense of entitlement they have and then turn around and insist on having everything about church be the way *they* think it should be from carpet, to hymns, to who is allowed in the pews.

I listen to people who tell me that social justice is not part of the church and it is a shame I cannot work for a mission house or a ministry, yet they claim to be a Christ-follower. Christ did the work of social justice, preached and taught the work of social justice, and gave us the finest example of social justice we could possibly receive. He ate with sinners, talked to those who were hated and abhorred, touched the lepers, was kind to the prostitutes, elevated the status of women and children and stressed the importance of caring for them. Jesus told the rich to give all they had to the poor and spoke more about money than any other topic. Then he told us to love each other and to love God. Those two rules summed up the Law and that is what we were to do in life. He also told us that the poor would always be with us but that he would not be here physically anymore (Matthew 26:11). This was not to tell us that we would be alone or that the poor would always find excuses. It was to tell us that we are to be *his* hands, feet, and heart *in* this world. There will always be people who need to be cared for, eaten with, loved, and accepted.

CHAPTER 31

MOMMA

Brenda has been adopted by Lisa, the secretary of the church. When I moved away, Brenda wanted a woman who could take the place of, "Momma." Lisa is a big-hearted woman who loves to laugh and has more patience than anyone I know. She has taken in Brenda and her baby and helps them cope with day-to-day life. They are flourishing under her love, care, and attention. I stopped in one day to visit and got to see all three of them at once! Brenda asks Lisa if she is a success story. As any true mother would respond, Lisa says, "Yes, you are."

CHAPTER 32

I WILL BE WITH YOU ALWAYS

I had a funeral the other day. It was a simple private graveside service. I went to the cemetery early and was waiting for everyone to get there. I started walking among the tombstones reading names, straightening decorations, and praying for the family and friends when I noticed something that stopped me in my tracks. The image was so striking that it left a profound impact on me. In the midst of the tombstones, plastic flowers, wilting flowers, fresh

flowers, knick-knacks, and symbols of life, death, love, family, forgotten, lost, and remembered, stood a statue of Jesus. He stood in silent guard over a tombstone. His red and white robe showing signs of age and dirt and weather. His face had become chipped and yet the kindness and love the artist tried to depict still showed.

As I looked at him, I wondered, "Where are his hands?"

Then I realized, "His hands are amongst the living, not the dead."

Chapter 33

Essay on Labels

I am constantly struck by the irony in how we label ourselves and others in order to identify and describe. We associate what we do with who we are, and there are some significant problems with that. We associate our worthiness by how we can label ourselves. Women are less than men. White is better than black. Rich is better than poor. Middle-class is squeezed. A banker is deferred to when a janitor is not. We label people as truants, homeless, gay, abominations, handsome, Asian, etc., etc.

Who is the person we are describing? The *real* person. Are they creative, intelligent, funny, compassionate? We lose that when we use the common labels we use.

The only purpose labels have is so we know who we can throw away and who we should impress. Think about that. It is actually socially and even religiously acceptable to throw away certain people – except that it is not acceptable. Are you religious or are you so filled with the love of God that labels mean nothing to you? Do you see the person? Do you love that person?

We take it further in that we also use labels to degrade ourselves and allow others to throw us away too. We are **ALL** worthy of love, acceptance, and grace. No labels. Period.

Chapter 34

How It All Began

When I first started as a local pastor nine years ago, I was the first female pastor that Belmont UMC had ever had. Due to a series of unexpected events, the appointment process had not followed the usual pattern and we had not met each other yet. They were anxious and unsure of who they were getting and I was walking into my first appointment without knowing them, their history, or what it was exactly that I was supposed to do. My first sermon changed when I realized they needed to talk about all that had happened and how they felt about having a young unmarried female pastor. I sat back and let them talk, deciding that their need to be heard was the most pressing issue at hand. After they had debated a little while, one of the church women stood up and said, "We need to remember that if the Lord can use an ass, He can surely use a woman." Thus began my journey into a life a ministry!

While attending seminary, I served that charge for four years. After graduating, I was appointed to Christ United Methodist Church as the Pastor of Parish Life. While there I immersed myself in social justice and pastoral care. I also travel to give talks based on my book, *Victim No More!* and book signings. I am a networker and look for who I can plug in where so I am always plugging people from the church into various programs in the church or the community. I have become pastor to many kinds of people and have encountered many types of settings I was not expecting. I learned that sometimes being a pastor entails protecting one person, kicking another person out of the church, having set-tos with abusive spouses and locking horns with those who stand in opposition. I have stood nose to nose with drug dealers, irate panhandlers, and have earned a bit of a reputation among the homeless folk in town as a kind minister who would help but who was also a hard ass.

Robert Wong, a church member who had a deep love for those in poverty, loved the fact that I was in the martial arts and loved my *Victim No More!* talks. He was a staunch supporter of whatever I got in to as he also was passionate about social justice. One day he started to question me about karate wanting to know if we fought "for real." He was awed by the fact that we only use light padding on hands and feet and actually make contact with each other. He loved it that I had black eyes and bloody noses. He called me his Reverend Bad Ass and introduced me that way to everyone he thought I should meet. At his funeral, I told the story of what he called me and about 600 people laughed. The feeling in the room changed from one of dread and despair to one of celebration as a life lived passionately and joyfully was remembered. Reverend Bad Ass is known more than Reverend Shauna Hyde, and Reverend Bad Ass was called when people needed to talk and grieve. There have been places in Charleston where I have been and no one knew who Shauna Hyde was but when they were told I was Reverend Bad Ass, they all went, "Oh! Hi!" I have been walking across a parking lot and heard someone yelling, "Hey, Reverend Bad Ass!" and just laughed and waved even if I had no clue who it was.

One day out of sheer curiosity, I began to research the whole ass/donkey topic and found some wonderfully interesting facts, legends, poems, etc. that made me realize the kind of pastor God is shaping me to be. I am not going to cite sources as I did no serious research and found the same information on the several websites. I just Google'd ass, jackass, and donkey to see what would come up. I learned that ass is the shortened version of the species name and became a form of profanity over the years when used as an insult. I learned that donkeys, AKA asses, are pretty cool animals. They are strong, dependable, companionable, and are actually not stubborn, contrary to popular myth. Farmers get donkeys to be companions for horses who are old, sick, or lonely because the donkey will care for them, lead them, and never leave their side. Racehorses that have lost their spirit are often paired with a donkey because the donkey will care for the racehorse and invigorate them again. Donkeys are also known for their sure-footedness, even when carrying a heavy load. Donkeys can tolerate a lot of adverse conditions, heavy burdens, heat, cold, little food, and cantankerous horses and humans.

When I started to put together Reverend Bad Ass with donkeys I began to see how my ministry is taking shape and who I have become. I am strong and have learned over the years how to carry heavy loads, how to be a companion to those who are sick, lonely, or beat down. I work hard to be dependable and do as I need to do and to provide safe spaces for people. As a pastor I am called to lead by teaching, preaching, encouraging, and serving. According to 1 Corinthians 13, I do that by loving and not by braying. I am to care for and invigorate those around me, especially the ones who have lost their desire to fly. God needs me to be sure-footed and to lead people on the path that would bring them closer to God. I become and stay sure-footed by spending time with God and listening for direction then obeying the direction God has given me.

I don't know how this story will end. I do know that God is calling me to be Reverend Bad Ass because God has placed me in a place where Reverend Bad Ass is who was needed for some people who are unchurched, de-churched, or just plain

cynical about the image of God they have pictured over the years. The church matriarch was more correct than she ever thought because if God can use an ass, He can surely use a Reverend Bad Ass.

CHAPTER 35

WHY? WHY NOT?

The Chairperson of the Trustees emailed me a few months ago. He understood what it felt like when I sat in front of the committee and defended my decision to move the Tent Town into the church building. He had rallied some people to build tent platforms in Tent Town and had met with resistance and people asking why that should be done. He did it anyway.

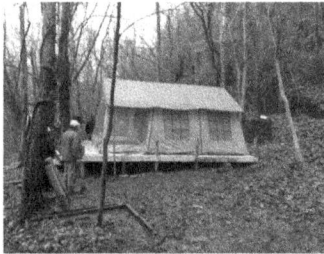

Chapter 36

Asking the Wrong Questions

People ask why the people in Tent Town don't just get a place to live, why they don't get a job, why they have no self-respect. They do not realize how long it takes to work less than 35 hours a week, stay fed, pay for transportation and save up for a security deposit, first month's rent, and utility deposits. If they ever get the money saved, they still have no food, no furniture, and none of the items to set up a home. That is if they do not get discouraged and just settle into their tent for the long-term.

CHAPTER 37

THE DONKEY MOVES ON

I was at a church leadership conference in Florida when I received the phone call from my District Superintendent about taking a church in Ravenswood, WV. I struggled to know what to do as I didn't feel like it was time to move yet. So, I spent a night in prayer and said, "God, You know me. I am a billboard kind of gal. I need this to be obvious. If I am to go, in tomorrow's worship service let someone lay their hand on my shoulder and pray specifically for me."

We attended the worship service and there were lots of moments of prayer but no one laid a hand on my shoulder and prayed specifically for me. I was starting to get a little happy thinking I was not going to move. Then at the very end of the service, the minister stood up and said, "We are going to end differently today. Lay your hand on the shoulder of the person next to you and pray with me, 'May the Lord bless you and keep you; may his face shine upon you and bring you peace.'

I was going to Ravenswood, West Virginia.

I returned home and told the church. They wept and hugged me and the choir sang the benediction, *May the Lord Bless You.*

I packed the house and headed the car north following the moving van. It was time to be the Lord's donkey somewhere else.

CHAPTER 38

HUNGER GAMES:
FRIDGE WARS

There has been much excitement here in Ravenswood, WV, and people have asked me to offer my insights and thoughts on the hubbub. I cannot remember how, when or who but a grass-roots idea came up about putting a fridge outside the church. We looked up USDA and FDA laws and discovered that we were on private property and that we were not cooking, handling raw foods, selling, etc. and we were assured that it would be okay. We built a "cage" inside the unit to prevent a child from being able to crawl inside and get trapped. So, the fridge was placed outside the church and filled with bottled water, juice, and Gatorade. People bought individually wrapped pieces of string cheese, boxes of raisins, even cans of food went in and we waited to see what would happen.

Why put a fridge outside? There are several reasons. We often look at "those people" who are hungry and poor and make their decisions for them. When going to a food pantry and other places that provide help, people have to put aside their dignity and take what is given. They have to let someone into their private lives and business and swallow their pride to ask for help. A fridge outside, allows dignity of choice and privacy.

Many older people are not able to make ends meet and they would rather starve than to let someone know that they were hungry. They were raised in a world that said you must work hard, take care of yourself and your family and it is shameful to not be able to accomplish something as simple as having food in the house.

In West Virginia, the number one form of child abuse is neglect. If a child can walk down the street to the local church and get a little something to eat, they won't go to bed hungry that night.

Many people who are hungry fall into what we call "the working poor." They cannot get to food pantries before they close because they *are* working. They also often fall into a group of people who make too much to receive help but not enough to make ends meet.

A fridge outside is a symbol of hope, of love, of being cared about, of being seen and acknowledged, and that God's people care so maybe – just maybe – God does too.

So, what happened? Well, someone called the Health Department. At first I could believe that it was truly a concerned individual but with the way it has escalated I have come to believe it is someone with a personal vendetta against either me or this particular church, or churches in general.

The Health Department called on a Monday. I assured them there was no prepared food in the fridge. Everything was sealed, dated, store-bought, etc. They called again. This time an unmanned fridge could not be kept in a public place. It is private property. They said I could move the fridge to the porch on my home but not at the church. My thought was, "????????" I waited. The fridge was emptied and refilled twice in a two week period. People needed food.

The Health Department came to the church the following Friday and informed us that we had to move the fridge indoors by Monday. At this point, I just started laughing. Apparently, they had received complaints every day. My guess is that it is all by the same person. So, I did not move it. Not only did I not move it, but a reporter contacted me (I had been posting the story on Facebook and it spread). A friend from another church I served in years ago contacted me as well. He also works in Health and did not understand what all the hubbub was about. He said he would contact this Health Department and try to understand and explain to me what was going on. So, now I am waiting.

People in the church have come to me repeatedly with messages of support telling me to not move the fridge. I have been sent emails, Facebook messages, and notes that say that I am supported in keeping a fridge outside the church.

I will do what I need to do to maintain health codes and to keep people safe. The Health Department is just doing their job. So am I. My job is "to make disciples of Jesus Christ for the transformation of the world" (UMC mission statement). My job is to feed the hungry, clothe the naked, visit the prisoners, and be the hands, heart, head, and feet of God in this world (begin with Matthew 25 and move on to other love your neighbor scriptures).

So, where are we and what will happen? Well, we will see. Right now, the fridge stays. I am praying that whoever is egging this on for their own agenda stops it when they realize the bigger picture. Every town has children who are hungry. We live in denial but it is often the child who lives beside us. If every church put a fridge outside and stocked it with healthy easy to open and eat foods, we could put a huge dent in the percentage of children and elderly who go to bed hungry every night. Such a simple act of love, grace, and hospitality really could transform the world.

CHAPTER 39

THE HUNGER GAMES:
FRIDGE FINALE

We gain strength, and courage, and confidence by each experience in which we really stop to look fear in the face... we must do that which we think we cannot. — Eleanor Roosevelt

We have all waited with baited breath to see what would happen. The local health inspector came and helped us set up the fridge in as safe a way as possible for people to use. Now we are challenged with keeping it stocked and prepared for those who need it. These kinds of challenges help us to grow as we realize that we could waste our money on something we do not need or help to stock a fridge with food that someone may desperately need. It sits in a storage shelter on the front porch of the church. It is regularly filled, emptied, and refilled. Teenagers playing basketball in the parking lot stop and get water, children running by stop and get a juice, mothers with babies in strollers stop to get a little something for dinner that night and the caretaker for an elderly man comes and finds a little food to help stretch the money to last through the week. Those who fill it do not give out of their wealth but out of their own need. Every Sunday, I ask the congregation to share where they have seen God in the last week. There is a regular answer of, "at the fridge."

We have to do quite a bit: we have to place it on a fiberglass mat, build a weather protection wall, keep a thermometer in place and check it daily, put up appropriate signage and we do have to padlock it at night. Some people are struggling with the padlock; however, we can post the hours on the fridge and keep them late enough in the evening and early enough in the morning to try to accommodate people. I know their concern stems from the possibility that someone could tamper with the food when no one is watching and people could get sick. So, we will lock it at night, keep a temperature log and work with them in making it safe. It took courage on the part of the inspectors to help sanction something so unusual! This is fantastic!!!

Imagine if every church had a fridge outside filled with store-bought, sealed, non-spoiled, nutritious food for anyone and everyone to help themselves to. Imagine the peace we could give to a worried mother, the second wind we could give to a worn-out father, and the love we could give to the child who thinks no one cares or the senior citizen who does not want anyone to know they are struggling.

Our parking lot often has kids and teenagers in it. They can help themselves. Many people use our parking lot to turn around in, to drive though, and to loop around in. It is used as a park and ride, a lunch break location, and a meeting place for chit chats. They can help themselves. We have a community garden on one side of the lot full of fresh produce and a fridge on the other side of the lot filled with bottled drinks, canned meats (the only kind of meat we can put in the fridge), boxes of raisins, fruit cups, string cheese sticks, and the list goes on.

I say that next we should put in a shelter with picnic tables and benches so that people do not have to sit in their cars to eat and talk but could get out and stretch their legs.

Some people want to know what will happen if we fail. I have laughed at that question because what would failing look like? If we have fed one person, we have succeeded.

People have declared that we will be vandalized and that bad things may happen. True. There will always be bad things that happen in any situation. We will clean it up and keep going. We also need to give the benefit of the doubt whenever possible. I have seen people rise to a better standard repeatedly in my lifetime. Let's offer them another opportunity.

The point to any plan or idea is to try. I would rather try and fail than to never try. Failure does not define a person, a group, or a plan. It is just part of the learning curve that allows us to make something better!

We are doing what has been asked of us and soon we will have it completed and others can do the same. We will all learn better ways and share them with each other. We will all discover that there will be different kinds of problems. We will share them with each other and help each other improve.

Meanwhile, I am working on other projects to help offer opportunities in the community for healing and hope. What can you do in your community? Will you put a fridge outside? If you will, let me know so we can work together and share ideas. Let's put a fridge in every part of town we can to tell the world that God sees them and loves them. Who's with me? [#fridgesforfriends]

The 24 hours which brought resolution were so good I just sit and cry for a minute as I remember. The community garden's yielding great produce. The fridge is set up and available. We are now in partnership with First Baptist church to help with their weekly free meal, and then the last bit of news: the Independent Freewill Baptist church minister and the North UMC minister and I have been working at bringing recovery ministries into town. One thing we really wanted was to be in partnership with a counseling center and to have a crisis center here in town. We will be able to house it out of First UMC. Everything is in place and ready to go when a counselor is in place at the center. An experienced counselor has expressed interest in being the counselor here at the church. I just sat and cried with sheer joy and thankfulness. God is in town, folks! Help, healing, and hope are being rained down on this town!

Chapter 40

Do You Love Me?

Jesus asked, "Do you love me?"
I replied, "With all my heart."
Jesus said, "Feed my sheep."
He asked again, "Do you love me?"
I replied, "Of course I do."
"Feed my sheep."
He asked again, "Shauna, do you love me?"
I replied, "Lord, you know I do."
Jesus said, "Love them with me. Hug them and hold them.
    Lift them up. Clothe them. Feed them."
I replied, "Yes. Lord."

Epilogue

This book has not been easy to write. I am the sort that seldom really lets people in to see the depth of me. The longer I am in ministry, the harder I have to struggle to not become completely disillusioned with humanity, Christianity, and the church universal. We have wandered too far off the path and forgotten that we are to love the hell out of people, not scare the hell out of people. We have forgotten that our issues are small in comparison with so many others. We have the luxury of fighting over theological controversies because we are not fighting for our lives. I work hard and pray hard to keep my heart full of love and compassion even if I do not express it in ways that people traditionally expect of a pastor.

I am blessed to be called to walk into holy places and holy moments every day of my life. I have enough stories to write multiple books on as I have traversed river banks, shelters, addiction centers, churches, and people's homes. The pain that people live with is real and is usually deeper and more significant that many of us will ever know. I am one of the trusted few that people will open up to. People will tell me their stories, show me their scars, and trust me to hold them as sacred. I have been blessed in this life. I take my role as treasure keeper seriously and I hold each person and confidence close to my heart.

I do struggle to love and show grace. I have been told repeatedly that love and grace are my spiritual gifts but often I do not feel like they are. The older I get and the more people I work with the harder it is for me to be patient with those who are intolerant and stuck in the myths and excuses of our society. I struggle to be accepting and understanding when organizations refuse to work together because an issue is more important than people. I become angry, distressed, and depressed when churches cannot put differences aside in order to transform the loves of those who are desperate to feel the touch of God. I can say that I have had upscale dinners with the wealthy and split a sandwich under a bridge with the not so wealthy. I can say I have had lunch with movie stars and I have rocked a homeless man to sleep. I have been at both ends of the spectrum and have seen the beauty that makes up humanity. Just when I think I am done and cannot love anymore because I am tired of the games people play and the silly things they get upset about, someone will show me the beauty of their souls – the place where God is and I know I can still love and show grace.

It is hard for me to remember that not everyone cares as much as I do – not because they are callous or apathetic but because they have not been given the opportunity to step outside their lives and truly become a part of the life of another. They see prejudice and poverty and other ways of life as abstract issues that they have opinions about, not as situations that devastate lives and people. This is why relationships are so important. Instead of serving a meal to the homeless, sit and eat with them. Instead of just handing them money, have a conversation. Instead of assuming to know, sit and listen. Instead of hating, choose love.

As a society, we have become self-centered to the point of being completely unaware of what the people around us are going through. When we do find out, we judge and gossip instead of love and listen; yet, everywhere I go in ministry, I find those people who quietly go about serving and reaching out with kind hands and gentle hearts. They just don't get as much attention as those who are being loud in order to detract others from noticing their own flaws. We have become more and more polarized over the perceived flaws of others, to the point that we constantly repel each other instead of moving forward together. This distresses me to no end. We can "be right" or we can love other people and be in relationship with them. We can pass judgment or we can raise others up. We can put down or we can lighten the load. It worries me a great deal that we still perpetuate myth and commonly held biases instead of getting to know people and hearing their stories.

It is always humbling to realize that any of us could end up differently than expected. Life changes quickly and people make the best choices they can. The challenge lies in accepting a choice different than our own instead of judging it.

We put up walls to protect ourselves and then have no boundaries in place. And we wonder why we have unhealthy relationships. We do not realize what a luxury that is. I learned from being around the homeless everyday that they have no walls up but they do enforce boundaries. Once they know they can trust you, they share their soul in ways that most of us never would. They strip bare and are unafraid of being naked in public. The pretense is gone. The fear of what other people may think is gone. There is no desire to impress, only to connect. There is no desire to hate or to judge only to be accepted. We can learn a lot from the homeless. I sometimes wonder if that factors in to why Jesus became homeless for his ministry. He was not held back by anything – there were no walls.

Updates

Adam

A friend has been going diligently to Tent Town to offer aid and to advocate for them as needed. She met Adam there. He has been sober long enough to receive housing. He has had his own apartment for one week. He still goes to Tent Town daily to check on the cats to make sure they have been fed and cared for. Many people leave animals by the river when they no longer want them. They become the pets and family members of those who reside there. There is hope walking the river bank of the Elk River.

Melissa

In one of my visits back to Charleston I saw a girl who looked familiar. Her eyes sparkled and danced and her smile came quick and easily. Her joy was contagious and she came over to hug me and to introduce me to her boyfriend of two years and their new baby. As the baby cooed and gurgled, her father wrapped his arm around her mother and looked at me with all the solemnity of young love. "I will take care of them and love them. I will do right by them." He shook my hand and looked me in the eye. Melissa's smile said it all. She had found someone who saw her beauty and vowed to love her. She bubbled over with plans for the future as the beaten down girl of yesterday faded further and further away.

Victim No More!

Full of spiritual instructions and practical wisdom, this book will make a person spiritually and physically fit and ready for life challenges. It is a trailblazing book. Highly recommended!

Andrew S. Park
Professor of Theology and Ethics
United Theological Seminary,
Dayton, OH

Shauna Hyde

$9.99 – STUDY GUIDES INCLUDED

QUANTITY DISCOUNTS AVAILABLE.

For those who seek a faith-based exploration of the dynamics of dysfunctional relationships, and suggestions how to improve one's self and one's interactions with others, this volume is ideal.

Ariana J. Kincaid
Violence Against Women
Resource Prosecutor
West Virginia Prosecuting
Attorneys Institute

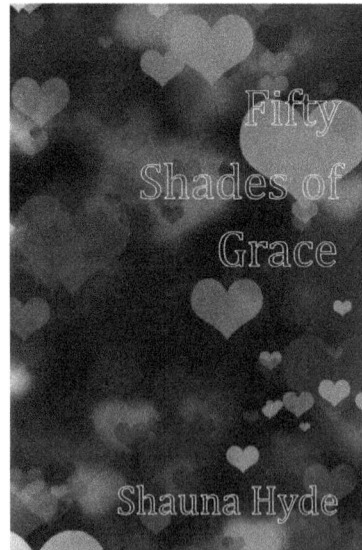

Fifty Shades of Grace

Shauna Hyde

Personal Study

Holy Smoke! Unholy Fire	Bob McKibben	$14.99
The Jesus Paradigm	David Alan Black	$17.99
When People Speak for God	Henry Neufeld	$17.99
The Sacred Journey	Chris Surber	$11.99

Christian Living

It's All Greek to Me	David Alan Black	$3.99
Grief: Finding the Candle of Light	Jody Neufeld	$8.99
My Life Story	Becky Lynn Black	$14.99
Crossing the Street	Robert LaRochelle	$16.99
Life as Pilgrimage	David Moffett-Moore	14.99

Bible Study

Learning and Living Scripture	Lentz/Neufeld	$12.99
From Inspiration to Understanding	Edward W. H. Vick	$24.99
Philippians: A Participatory Study Guide	Bruce Epperly	$9.99
Ephesians: A Participatory Study Guide	Robert D. Cornwall	$9.99
Ecclesiastes: A Participatory Study Guide	Russell Meek	$9.99

Theology

Creation in Scripture	Herold Weiss	$12.99
Creation: the Christian Doctrine	Edward W. H. Vick	$12.99
The Politics of Witness	Allan R. Bevere	$9.99
Ultimate Allegiance	Robert D. Cornwall	$9.99
History and Christian Faith	Edward W. H. Vick	$9.99
The Journey to the Undiscovered Country	William Powell Tuck	$9.99
Process Theology	Bruce G. Epperly	$4.99

Ministry

Clergy Table Talk	Kent Ira Groff	$9.99
Out of This World	Darren McClellan	$24.99

Generous Quantity Discounts Available
Dealer Inquiries Welcome
Energion Publications — P.O. Box 841
Gonzalez, FL_ 32560
Website: http://energionpubs.com
Phone: (850) 525-3916

www.ingramcontent.com/pod-product-compliance
Lightning Source LLC
Chambersburg PA
CBHW031629040426
42452CB00007B/746